# Dinosaur BUILDER

**Rob Waring,** *Series Editor*

HEINLE
CENGAGE Learning™

Australia • Brazil • Japan • Korea • Mexico • Singapore • Spain • United Kingdom • United States

# Words to Know

This story is set in Canada.
It takes place near Niagara Falls
in the province of Ontario
[ɒntɛəriou].

 **Dinosaurs.** Read the paragraph. Then write the basic form of each underlined word next to the correct definition.

Dinosaurs dominated the earth for over 160 million years. Some of these amazing reptiles were quite small, while others were absolutely enormous. Because they are now extinct, much of what scientists know about these animals that roamed our planet so long ago comes from the study of fossils and ancient dinosaur skeletons found underground.

**1.** the remains of ancient animal or plant life preserved in rock: _____
**2.** a type of animal that lived millions of years ago: _____
**3.** wander; move around freely: _____
**4.** a body's bones: _____
**5.** no longer in existence: _____
**6.** a group of cold-blooded animals that have backbones, live on land and usually produce young by laying eggs: _____

**Ancient Fossils**

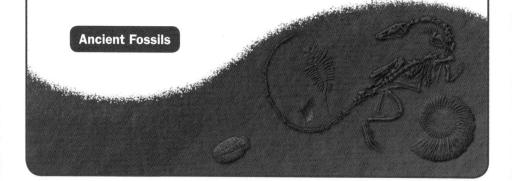

## B Building Dinosaurs. Read the paragraph. Then match each word with the correct definition.

Peter May's job is to recreate dinosaurs for museum displays. His workshop is full of artificial dinosaur skeletons that will someday be mounted in museums around the world. In order to make them, Peter and his team of craftsmen and women first examine the work of palaeontologists to learn about the animal they're going to make. Then, they make casts of the real bones in order to create artificial ones. The artificial bones are made of fibreglass to ensure that they are both strong and lightweight.

| | |
|---|---|
| **1.** recreate _____ | **a.** a skilled person, especially one who makes beautiful items by hand |
| **2.** workshop _____ | **b.** a strong, light material made from glass and plastic |
| **3.** mount _____ | **c.** a building or area with machinery and tools |
| **4.** craftsman/ woman _____ | **d.** a scientist who studies fossils and bones |
| **5.** palaeontologist _____ | **e.** put on display; hang up |
| **6.** cast _____ | **f.** make something from the past exist again |
| **7.** fibreglass _____ | **g.** an object made by pouring hot liquid into a container and cooling it to copy a specific shape |

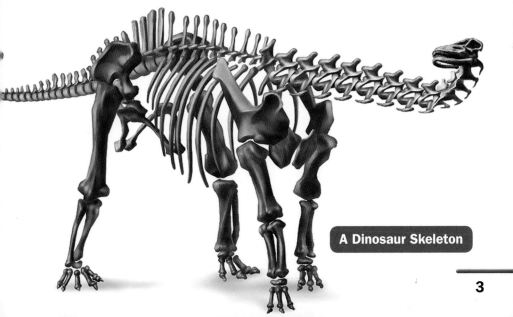

**A Dinosaur Skeleton**

Even before the days of Hollywood's big hit dinosaur films, museum dinosaur displays have long been something that fascinated children and adults alike. These mysterious reptiles that roamed the earth millions of years ago have kept people's interest for years. The enormous skeletons of dinosaurs seen in museums often fill viewers with amazement and wonder as they wander through the huge halls. However, few people likely consider who makes these incredible creations, and more importantly how. Constructing these fascinating museum displays is actually a unique combination of art, **craft**[1] and science, and it requires a combination of skills that very few have mastered.

Perhaps the top dinosaur builder in the world is a Canadian craftsman called Peter May. It's his job to reconstruct the huge dinosaur skeletons found by palaeontologists and he does it in his workshop not far from Niagara Falls, Ontario. Here, May creates these amazing reminders of life on our Earth millions of years ago and sends them to museums all around the world. Obviously, it's not a quiet art studio filled will paper and paint; it's a huge open room full of machines and various types of equipment needed to make these amazing creations. It also houses several half-finished dinosaur skeletons as well. For some, May's busy workshop may seem a bit like a 'dinosaur building site' with a diverse collection of ancient beasts in the process of being brought back to life.

---

[1]**craft:** a job or activity requiring skill or experience in making things

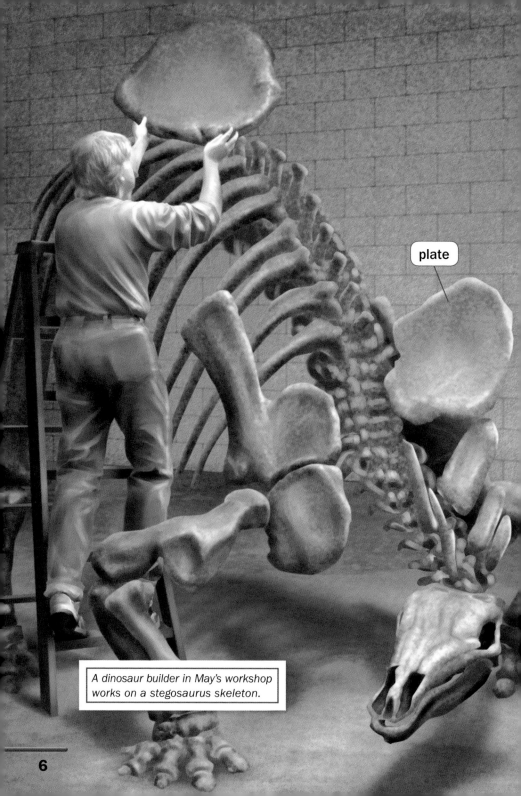

plate

A dinosaur builder in May's workshop works on a stegosaurus skeleton.

The workshop bursts with noise and activity – and parts of dinosaurs. They hang from the ceiling, sit on large tables, and are transported around the huge facility by large pieces of construction equipment. There are backbones as long as buses, legs as tall as small trees and heads almost as big as cars. Above them all, one can find terrifying half-finished flying creatures from the distant past hanging in the air, almost as if ready to come to life.

In one corner there's a semi-complete skeleton of a dinosaur that's almost as big as a house. As he stands near the tail of the huge prehistoric beast, May describes the piece. 'It's a work in progress on a stegosaurus,' he explains, placing his hand gently on the giant skeleton, 'and we haven't put the **plates**[2] on it yet or reconstructed the backbone.' He then talks about the complexity level of the project adding, 'This one is pretty **straightforward**.[3] It's your old standard dinosaur.'

Recreating a stegosaurus may be a straightforward task if you're Peter May – but that's because he's one of the world's best at this craft. Most people would find building a dinosaur an extremely difficult task, and very few would have the chance to attempt it at all. May explains that even his introduction into the job was a bit arbitrary; he didn't exactly plan to have a career building dinosaurs. 'This came right **out of the blue**,'[4] he laughs. 'It's just grown. I don't think anybody could sit down in their late teens and say "I'm going to be a dinosaur builder."'

---

[2]**plate:** a flat sheet of hard material; in this case the vertical body parts that protected the backbone of the stegosaurus
[3]**straightforward:** clear, direct; without complications
[4]**out of the blue:** *(expression)* occurring randomly with no warning

The story of how Peter May became a dinosaur builder is an interesting topic, one which actually grew out of staff problems at the world's museums. May began his career working at Toronto's Royal Ontario Museum in the early 1980s. Later, however, many of the museums around the globe could no longer afford to keep experts like May on their staff since they often only need a new display every few decades. This is how the Canadian dinosaur builder found the job that seemed suited for him. Instead of limiting himself to one museum that wouldn't always need his help putting up new displays, he started hiring himself out as a **freelancer**.[5] That way any museum in the world could contract him to mount a display when they needed him rather than employ a full-time dinosaur builder. Before long, May became very busy.

Kevin Seymour of the Royal Ontario Museum explains how May does it. 'So, he found that if he freelanced, then the museums of the world could come to him when they needed him,' he says. 'And that's what's happening. He has jobs in Europe and in Japan and all around the world.' Seymour adds, 'Most people believe he's the best.' Looking at the amount of work in his workshop, being the best has obviously helped May's business.

---

[5]**freelancer:** someone who works as an independent, self-employed person performing jobs for a variety of companies

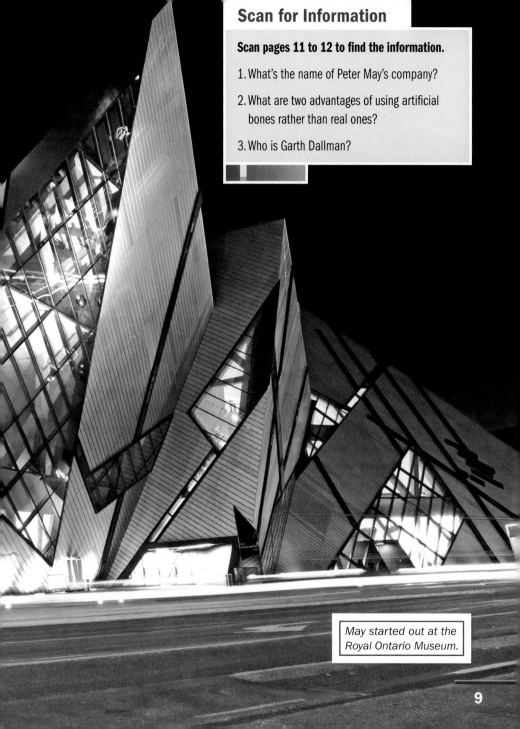

## Scan for Information

**Scan pages 11 to 12 to find the information.**

1. What's the name of Peter May's company?

2. What are two advantages of using artificial bones rather than real ones?

3. Who is Garth Dallman?

*May started out at the Royal Ontario Museum.*

It's rare for May's company, Research Casting International, or RCI, to mount actual dinosaur bones. Most of their work involves making casts of the real bones in order to create artificial ones. The basic process begins with painting the actual bone with a coat of rubber to recreate the look, feel and shape of a real dinosaur bone. Next, the workers wrap the cast shape in a hard covering to support it. Lastly, they mix the fibreglass compound and pour it into the shape of the bone. The fibreglass displaces the air in the centre of the cast shape and when it dries, the finished product is an artificial bone that is identical in shape to the real one.

There are a number of advantages to using artificial bones when creating model skeletons for museum displays. These artificial bones are cheaper and lighter than the actual bones, which is advantageous to both parties involved in the process. It's an advantage to the museum in that it helps keep costs down and budgets under control. It's also helpful to the dinosaur builders because the reduced weight makes the bones easier to work with and the skeletons easier to mount for display. Another benefit of using artificial bones is the fact that holes can be drilled into them in order to mount them on the steel frameworks. This allows the skeletons to be assembled on central supporting structures, thus making them more stable. In addition, palaeontologists obviously prefer not to drill holes in the actual ancient bones as the drilling would damage them, thereby compromising an important link to our planet's past.

The work done by RCI is complicated and incredibly detailed, requiring great accuracy on the part of the dinosaur builders. Most of the skeletons being recreated are incomplete, which forces the builders to shape the missing parts themselves in order to recreate the skeletal components of an animal that has been extinct for millions of years. They accomplish this by using technical drawings of fossils and of the dinosaurs themselves as guides. It's the type of work in which it's critical to be accurate and the craftsmen and women can't deviate from the plans; they are tightly restricted to scientific reality. Unfortunately, there isn't exactly a 'Dinosaur Building Academy' or even many written guidelines or publications about how to mount dinosaurs. Therefore, with each display they construct May's team must learn on the job.

Some of May's team members have no background experience related specifically to dinosaur making or even to science. A few even started their careers in completely different jobs. One member, Garth Dallman, is a **blacksmith**[6] by trade. He explains that the skills he learned as a blacksmith have proved to be extremely relevant in reconstructing dinosaurs. Unfortunately, they're also skills that are not often useful in the outside business world anymore. Dallman explains: '[Being a dinosaur builder] is a good **blend**[7] of science and art. My skills are actually … I guess they're coming back in a lot of ways. Some people [want] decorative iron working, but the actual trade of blacksmithing is a bit of a dinosaur too.'

---

[6]**blacksmith:** a skilled worker who makes and fixes things made of iron
[7]**blend:** combination; a mixture of two or more things

Putting a dinosaur skeleton together is a natural version of a building project, but one in which everything must fit together like a giant **jigsaw puzzle**.[8] The unfortunate aspect of this puzzle is that if just one piece of the skeleton is placed incorrectly, the entire structure could be thrown out of shape. Kevin Prudek's job is to actually put the huge reptiles skeletons together. He explains: 'If you don't start with the leg in the right way, then the hip will be wrong and the backbone will be wrong. So you really have to know what you're doing from the beginning on so that everything works properly. I mean, it's like a puzzle. You can't put one piece in wrong and expect everything else to fit.'

---

[8]**jigsaw puzzle:** a form of entertainment in which a picture on paper or wood that has been cut into pieces is put back together

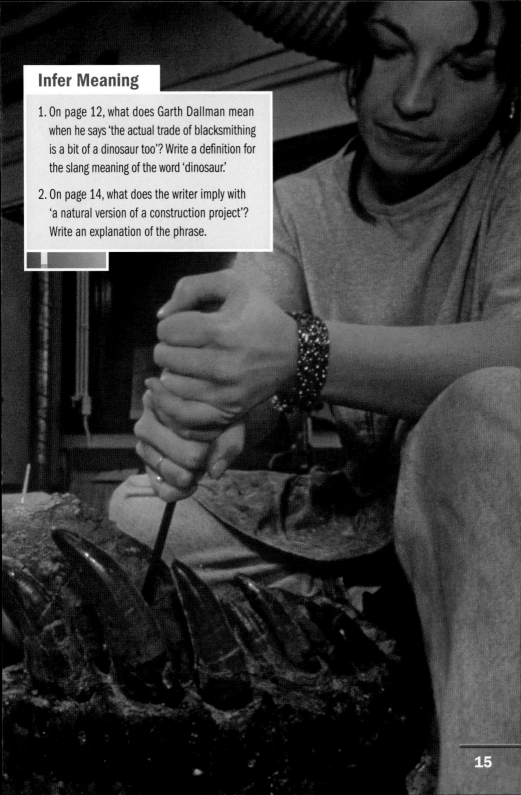

## Infer Meaning

1. On page 12, what does Garth Dallman mean when he says 'the actual trade of blacksmithing is a bit of a dinosaur too'? Write a definition for the slang meaning of the word 'dinosaur.'

2. On page 14, what does the writer imply with 'a natural version of a construction project'? Write an explanation of the phrase.

Pigeon

Archaeopteryx

Ornitholestes

The builders in May's workshop do much more than just build dinosaurs, however. They also help scientists solve the mysteries and **controversies**[9] surrounding these ancient creatures' appearance and behaviour. Since they roamed the earth long before humans did, there is no human record of them, and scientists can often only hypothesise as to the reality of the lives and actions of these giant beasts. Kevin Seymour explains just how crucial the quality and accuracy of mounting is to science. '[The dinosaur builders] are **in the fore[front]**[10] of the controversies of how these animals lived and acted,' he says, 'because how you put them together, what kind of **posture**[11] you put them in, really is the way they're interpreted. A palaeontologist might say "we believe it's done this way", and the guy who's mounting it could say, "I don't think the bones go together that way. Look." You know? So there is this conversation back and forth that's quite valuable.'

Seymour goes on to explain that the positioning, or 'posing,' of the dinosaurs when on display can place the mount on the level of art. It's important that the body is mounted correctly and looks natural as opposed to looking strange or out of proportion due to poor positioning. Seymour explains: 'There's a very big difference between an average mount and a fantastic mount. A really beautifully posed mount is a work of art.' The level of respect received for a job well done seems to justify the amount of work needed to recreate the figure of one of these huge, ancient creatures.

---

[9]**controversy:** public disagreement, usually involving strong opinions and an important subject
[10]**in the forefront:** in the most important or noticeable position
[11]**posture:** the position in which the body is held by a person or animal

In addition to helping dinosaur displays to be considered art, the dinosaur builders are also the public face of palaeontology. They deal with the results, or the 'big show,' that follows all of the difficult work done by palaeontologists. They're the ones who discover and document the fossils and bones that tell us so much about the dinosaurs. The dinosaur builders are the ones who bring that history to life with their recreations of animals that have not walked the earth for millions of years.

Peter May describes what it's like to be involved in the work of constructing and mounting these ancient beasts. 'It's like anything. It becomes a **labour of love**,'[12] he declares. 'These guys were **king of the hill**[13] back then, you know? As you work on it, **your mind drifts**[14] and then when it's mounted, it's on display in a museum, one skeleton becomes a part of the whole, which is the history of our world.' It's obvious that educating people about the animals that once dominated all others is something that this dinosaur builder both loves and respects.

---

[12] **labour of love:** *(expression)* a piece of work done for one's own pleasure or to please someone else, and not for money or other gain
[13] **king of the hill:** *(expression)* the most important or powerful
[14] **(one's) mind drifts:** the mind or thoughts go in unexpected or unplanned directions

19

# After You Read

1. What is the purpose of the paragraph 1 on page 4?
   A. to introduce the topic of dinosaur building
   B. to explain why people are fascinated with dinosaurs
   C. to share details about the skeletons of dinosaurs
   D. to contrast the different dinosaurs in museums

2. From the information in paragraph 1 on page 7, it can be inferred that Peter May:
   A. is too busy to finish all his work
   B. needs to hire more employees
   C. has a busy, successful business
   D. gets complaints about noise from his neighbours

3. On page 7, the stegosaurus skeleton is given as an example of how:
   A. slowly Peter May must work
   B. Peter May views the complexity of his work
   C. Peter May exploits dinosaurs
   D. Peter May began his career

4. Which of the following summarises how Peter May became a dinosaur builder?
   A. It was a goal he pursued from a young age.
   B. He chose the right career after leaving school.
   C. He took advantage of an opportunity to work with several different museums.
   D. He wanted to find the best way to make the most money.

5. The size, cost and weight are reasons why artificial bones are better to use than real ones when building dinosaurs.
   A. True
   B. False
   C. Not in text

6. The word 'accuracy' in paragraph 1 on page 12 can be replaced by:
   A. tension
   B. convergence
   C. struggle
   D. precision

**7.** How did Research Casting International learn the trade so well?
   **A.** by attending a dinosaur-building academy
   **B.** through studying from textbooks
   **C.** Peter May taught each person individually
   **D.** through experience

**8.** Which of these statements best expresses the conclusion Garth Dallman draws on page 12?
   **A.** Blacksmiths could have existed at the same time as dinosaurs.
   **B.** Blacksmiths are mostly unnecessary in contemporary times.
   **C.** Blacksmiths are not treated fairly by the business world.
   **D.** Blacksmiths are artists, not scientists.

**9.** Which is an appropriate heading for page 14?
   **A.** Kevin Prudek Can't Solve Giant Puzzle
   **B.** Stegosaurus Bone Misplaced by Builders
   **C.** Skeleton Constructed Delicately and Carefully
   **D.** One Right Piece Means Everything Is Wrong

**10.** What does 'they' in 'they're' refer to in paragraph 1 on page 17?
   **A.** dinosaurs
   **B.** scientists
   **C.** skeletons
   **D.** builders

**11.** What opinion does Kevin Seymour express on page 17?
   **A.** Scientists have the best theories about how dinosaurs moved.
   **B.** Mounting can be done by anyone after the bones are built.
   **C.** Builders contribute valuable knowledge about dinosaurs.
   **D.** The most difficult part of building is finding the right posture.

**12.** It can be inferred that the writer thinks that dinosaur builders:
   **A.** connect the public to ancient history
   **B.** are too proud of their skeletons
   **C.** enforce the work of palaeontologists
   **D.** are more important than scientists

# New Science

## Dinosaur Debate

There are several differing theories about what happened to the dinosaurs. Scientists agree that about 50 per cent of all the plants and animals that existed on earth became extinct about 65 million years ago. They also agree that at a similar time, a huge piece of rock from outer space, called a 'meteorite,' landed in Mexico. Using this as a starting point, Doctor of Physics Luis Alvarez proposed the following theory: the impact of the meteorite was so strong that it caused enormous clouds of dirt and dust to cover the sky, blocking out the sun and causing the temperature on Earth to fall greatly. The result was called 'impact winter.' Followers of this theory believe that during this cool period, many types of plants died out, which in turn resulted in the extinction of many animals on Earth, including dinosaurs.

Other scientists have somewhat different interpretations of why the dinosaurs disappeared. Dewey McLean, a geologist at Virginia Polytechnic University, agrees that the impact caused severe changes in the earth's climate. However, he believes that the earth was already experiencing an overall rise in the temperature of its atmosphere called 'global warming.' He felt that this was due to extremely active volcanoes on the Indian subcontinent, which were spilling out vast quantities of melted rock, or lava, onto the earth's surface. Scientists believe that the lava covered

*Many scientists believe that a meteorite was at least in part responsible for the extinction of the dinosaurs.*

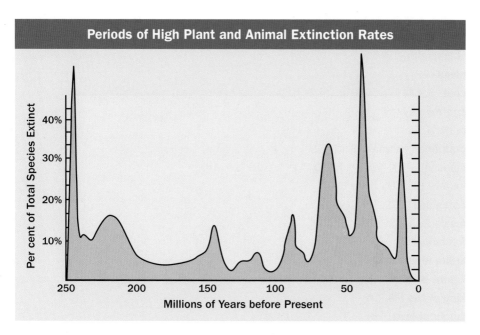

**Periods of High Plant and Animal Extinction Rates**

Per cent of Total Species Extinct

Millions of Years before Present

over a million square miles of India and the surrounding countries. McLean believes that this volcanic activity resulted in changes to the balance of chemicals in the air and the ocean water. He theorises that these changes contributed to the global extinction of plant and animal species because they could not survive the chemical changes in their environment.

Peter Ward, professor of geological sciences at the University of Washington in Seattle, adds his own view to those of earlier researchers. He agrees with Dr. McLean that dinosaurs did not become extinct because of a single meteorite impact. He also agrees that global warming, principally caused by volcanic activity, was the reason for their dying out. However, he suggests that volcanoes in northern Russia contributed to the changes in the climate. He points to scientific evidence showing that the process of extinction was a slow one, lasting millions of years, which indicates that it was not a sudden occurrence. Other scientists hold very different theories and it will probably be many years before the debate is resolved completely.

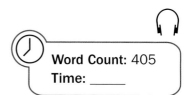

**Word Count:** 405
**Time:** _____

# Vocabulary List

**blacksmith** (12, 15)
**blend** (12)
**cast** (3, 11)
**controversy** (17)
**craft** (4, 7)
**craftsman/woman** (3, 4, 12)
**dinosaur** (2, 3, 4, 6, 7, 8, 11, 12, 14, 15, 17, 18)
**extinct** (2, 12)
**fibreglass** (3, 11)
**fossil** (2, 3, 12, 18)
**freelancer** (8)
**in the forefront** (17)
**jigsaw puzzle** (14)
**king of the hill** (18)
**labour of love** (18)
**mount** (3, 8, 11, 12, 17, 18)
**(one's) mind drifts** (18)
**out of the blue** (7)
**palaeontologist** (3, 4, 11, 17, 18)
**plate** (6, 7)
**posture** (17)
**recreate** (3, 11, 12, 17, 18)
**reptile** (2, 4, 14)
**roam** (2, 4, 17)
**skeleton** (2, 3, 4, 6, 7, 11, 12, 14, 18)
**straightforward** (7)
**workshop** (3, 4, 6, 7, 8, 17)